KT-215-817

C333736794

MOVING UP WITH SCIENCE

FORCES AND MAGNETS

Peter Riley

W
FRANKLIN WATTS
LONDON·SYDNEY

To my granddaughter, Holly Jane.

First published in 2015 by
Franklin Watts
338 Euston Road
London NW1 3BH

Franklin Watts Australia
Level 17/207 Kent Street
Sydney NSW 2000

Text copyright © Peter Riley 2015
Copyright images © Franklin Watts 2015

HB ISBN 978 1 4451 3523 6
Library ebook ISBN 978 1 4451 3524 3

Dewey classification number: 531'.133
All rights reserved.

A CIP catalogue record for this book is available from the British Library.

Editor: Hayley Fairhead
Designer: Elaine Wilkinson

Photo acknowledgements: Black Rock Digital p4b; Dan Van Den Broeke title page, p17,
p13; Yuriy Chaban cover inset; Andy Crawford p15; dragon_fang p8t; stuart.ford p12;
Jaroslav Frank p8b and p29; Rainer Junker p26 and p31; Miloszbudzynski cover main;
Ray Moller p4tl, p4tr, p5t, p6t, p6b, p7t, p16t, p16b, p20, p21, p22, p23t, p23b, p24t,
p24b; nathapol HPS p5bl; oneinchpunch p11; Paolo De Santis p9.

Artwork: John Alston

All other photographs by Leon Hargreaves.
With thanks to our models Layomi Obanubi, Sebastian Smith-Beatty and Sofia Bottomley.

Every attempt has been made to clear copyright. Should there be any inadvertent omission,
please apply to the Publishers for rectification.

Franklin Watts is a division of Hachette Children's Books, an Hachette UK company.
www.hachette.co.uk

Printed in China

Contents

Words in **bold** can be found in the glossary on pages 28–29.

What is a force?

A force is a push or a pull. You cannot see a force but you can see what happens when a force has been used. Some forces make things move.

When you kick a ball, a pushing force gets the ball moving.

When you take a book out of your bag, a pulling force moves the book up.

Push or pull?

Here are some more examples of pushes and pulls. Look at each picture carefully and decide whether a push or a pull has been used. You can see if you were right on page 5.

Brushing hair.

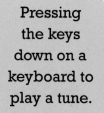

Making
a car
move.

Pressing
the keys
down on a
keyboard to
play a tune.

Putting
socks
on.

Were you right?

When you brush your hair, your hand pulls the brush through your hair. You push the toy car with your hand. If the car is a pull-back car, you might have pulled it instead. Your fingers push the keys down on a keyboard. Your hands pull your sock up your foot.

Close this book and then open it again. When did you use a push and when did you use a pull? Write a list of all the times you use a push and a pull during your day.

Squash, stretch, turn, twist

We use a pushing or pulling force in almost all the things we do. When we use a push or a pull we can change the shape of objects or move them by squashing, stretching, turning or twisting them.

Squashing

You squash a sponge ball or piece of clay by pushing it down with your hand.

A pushing force squashes this clay.

A pulling force stretches this elastic band.

Stretching

You stretch an elastic band as you pull it tight.

Turning

You turn a door handle by pushing it down. You turn the wheel on your bicycle by pushing down on the pedals. You push as you turn the key in a lock.

A pushing force turns this door handle.

Twisting

We use forces to twist things. You use a pushing force as you twist a bottle top onto a bottle, for example.

Seb pushes one way on the towel to twist it and Sofia pushes in the opposite direction.

Gravity

Look at this picture. What will happen to the balloon as Karen pushes her foot down?

A non-contact force

The push as Karen stamps down is too strong for the balloon. The balloon pops.

Another force pulls Karen's foot to the ground. This force is called **gravity**. Gravity is different from the other forces we have looked at. With other pushes and pulls, the forces touch the objects they are moving or changing. They are called **contact forces**. Gravity does not touch the object it is pulling. It is called a **non-contact force**.

Gravity is the force pulling bikes and their riders back to Earth.

The Earth

You might think that gravity pulls everything down to the **surface** of the Earth, but this is not really the case. Gravity pulls everything down to the centre of the Earth. This is why objects fall down holes. If we throw a pebble down a well, for example, the pebble falls right to the bottom.

Gravity from the Earth pulls on the Moon so that it moves around the Earth.

Earth

Moon

Gravity in space

Other **planets** and **stars** also have a **gravitational pull**. There is a pull of gravity between the Sun and the planets in the **Solar System**, for instance. It keeps the planets moving around the Sun.

Find two coins of different sizes and drop them from the same height onto a metal tray. Do they hit the tray together or at different times?

Friction

If you put a book at the top of a plank of wood and slowly start to tip the plank, you will see that at first the book stays still. It is held in place by a force between the book and plank. This force is called **friction**. As the book does not move, the friction is called **static** friction.

Sliding friction

There is a second force acting on the book. It is the force of gravity. Gravity acts to pull the book down the plank. On a gently sloping plank the force of static friction is strong enough to balance the pull of gravity and the book stays still. If the plank is tilted higher, the static friction is not strong enough and so the pull of gravity causes the book to slide. There is still friction between the book and the plank as the book moves. This friction is called **sliding friction**.

The more the plank is tipped, the greater the pull of gravity and the faster the book moves.

Friction and feet

When you walk your feet push on the ground to move you forwards. If you look at the soles of your bare feet with a magnifying glass you can see lines with grooves between them. These lines make a rough surface that builds up static friction between your foot and the ground and holds your foot steady as you move. But when your feet get wet, water fills the grooves and makes them smooth, reducing the static friction.

When your feet get wet, the force of static friction is reduced and your feet start to slip and slide.

Rub your hands together then put on some hand cream and rub again. What happens to your hands?

Investigating friction

You can investigate the strength of friction in different ways.

Testing friction with shoes

If you walk around a smooth, polished wood floor in your socks you may slip, but if you put on your trainers you will not. This difference is due to the friction between what's on your feet and the floor. Your sock is soft and smooth, while your trainer sole has lots of grooves.

When you wear trainers which have a greater force of static friction than your socks, you are less likely to slip over, even while running on smooth floors.

Trainers have lots of grooves and rough sections which make them good for gripping most surfaces.

Smooth, rough, bumpy

Different surfaces affect friction. You can investigate them by letting cars roll down ramps with different surfaces, such as a smooth plank of wood, rough sandpaper or foam, bumpy cardboard or scrunched-up paper. Gravity pulls the cars down the ramp. Friction between the car wheels and the ramp's surface slows the cars down. If three identical cars are placed at the top of the ramps and let go at the same time the picture below shows what will happen.

Equipment:

• three identical cars
• a smooth piece of wood with a strip of foam and a piece of bumpy cardboard attached

The car travels down the smooth wooden surface the fastest. The car travels down the rough foam surface the next fastest. The car travels down the bumpy cardboard surface the slowest.

On which surface in this experiment is the force of friction strongest? On which surface is the force of friction weakest? What does this experiment tell you about friction and speed?

13

Force fields

A force field is the place where a non-contact force can pull or push on things around it.

The Earth's force field

You are in the Earth's gravity force field. When you jump up, Earth's gravity pulls you back down.

Scientists believe that at the centre of the Earth there is a ball of solid iron and nickel. They think there is a ball of hot liquid iron and nickel around it. As the Earth turns on its **axis**, the solid iron ball spins in the hot liquid. This makes a **magnetic** force field around the Earth. The **North and South Poles** are the ends of the axis on which the Earth turns.

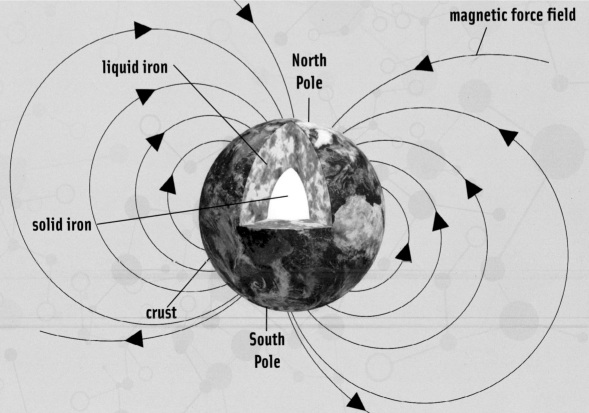

liquid iron

magnetic force field

North Pole

solid iron

crust

South Pole

Magnetic force field

Earth is a bit like a huge magnet. All magnets have force fields around them where they can pull on **magnetic materials**. The force field is strongest at the magnet's two **poles**. The pole is the place at the end of the magnet where the magnetic force comes from. Each magnet has a north and a south pole.

Tiny iron filings show the magnetic force field around this bar magnet. The filings have gathered around the poles where the force field is strongest. The plastic cover keeps the iron filings off the magnet.

Trace the picture of Earth shown on page 14 and draw a bar magnet inside it pointing to the North and South Poles. Draw the force field around the magnet, like the iron filings shown here.

Magnetic force

You can feel the power of a magnetic force with this quick experiment.

1.
Take the bar magnet in one hand and the steel spoon in the other hand and start to slowly move the two objects together. As you bring the spoon closer you might feel it wobble as the magnet's force begins to pull on it.

2.
The magnet's force will **attract** the spoon to the magnet. It also makes the spoon stick to the magnet.

Testing the magnetic force

Another way to test magnetic force is to put the spoon on the table. Hold the magnet over the spoon handle and start to lower it. When the magnet is very close, the magnetic force may pull the spoon handle towards the magnet. To take the spoon away from the magnet you have to pull them apart with both hands. Your pulling force must be stronger than the magnetic force to take the spoon away from the magnet.

Some magnets have a very strong magnetic force. They can lift huge pieces of metal.

What jobs could large magnets be used for?

Magnetic test

To see if all materials stick to magnets, try the following experiment with a collection of objects made from different materials. Which materials do you think will stick to the magnet?

Equipment:
- bar magnet
- copper scourer
- brass door knob
- iron pan
- plastic car
- aluminium foil
- steel bowl
- pottery mug
- any other objects made from different materials you can find

1.
Take a bar magnet and bring it near each of your chosen items in turn. If the magnet sticks to the material we say the material is a magnetic material. If the magnet does not stick to the material we say the material is a **non-magnetic material**.

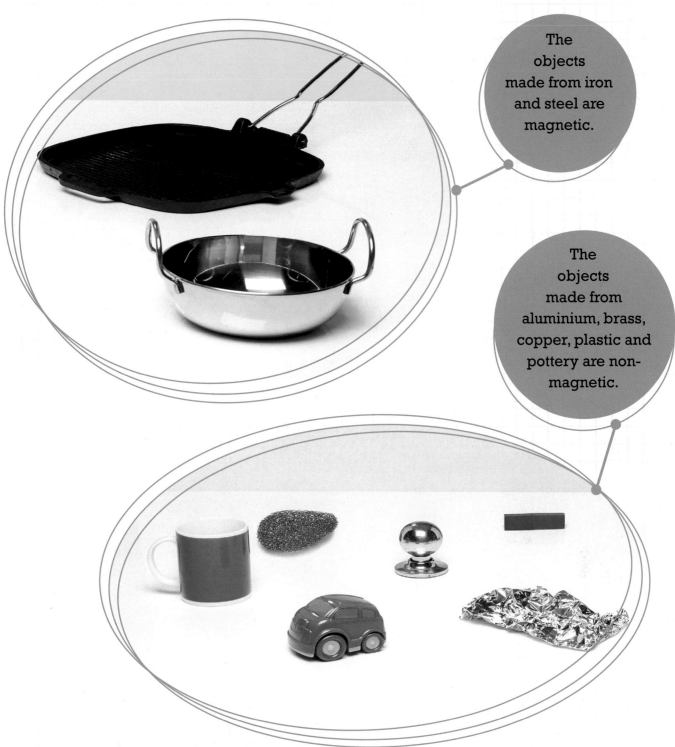

The
objects
made from iron
and steel are
magnetic.

The
objects
made from
aluminium, brass,
copper, plastic and
pottery are non-
magnetic.

Are all metals magnetic?

Experiments sometimes show surprising results. A metal is a hard
and often shiny material which lets electricity and heat pass through it.
Iron and steel are metals. When you test them with a magnet they stick
to it. They are magnetic materials. But not all metals are magnetic.
Copper, aluminium and brass are metals too and these are non-magnetic.

Magnetic poles

The Earth's magnetic force field is all around us. If a magnet is hung from a piece of string, it is free to move in the force field. When this happens, the Earth's force field pushes and pulls on the magnet until one end points towards the North Pole and the other end points towards the South Pole.

Repelling and attracting

Magnets have a north pole and a south pole where the magnetic pull is strongest. The north pole of this magnet is red and the south pole is blue.

Try these two experiments to find out what happens when the poles of two different magnets are brought together.

1.
Bring the north pole of the magnet in your hand close to the north pole of the hanging magnet. The north pole of the hanging magnet moves away. We say it is **repelled** by the north pole of the second magnet.

Equipment:

• bar magnet hung from piece of string
• bar magnet held in your hand

2.
Move the north pole of the magnet in your hand towards the south pole of the hanging magnet. The south pole of the hanging magnet will move towards the north pole of the second magnet. We say that it is attracted to the magnet's north pole.

N
S

N
S

Feeling the magnetic force

You do not need to hang up a magnet to see how the poles pull and push each other. You can simply bring two magnets together with your hands. You will soon see and feel the magnetic forces at work.

What do you think would happen if you brought two south poles together? Which poles attract each other – the opposite or the same? Which poles repel each other – the opposite or the same?

Finding the poles

There are many kinds of magnet. Bar magnets with red and blue ends show you their north and south poles. A horseshoe magnet does not have colours to show you its poles. You can find them by testing the horseshoe magnet with a bar magnet.

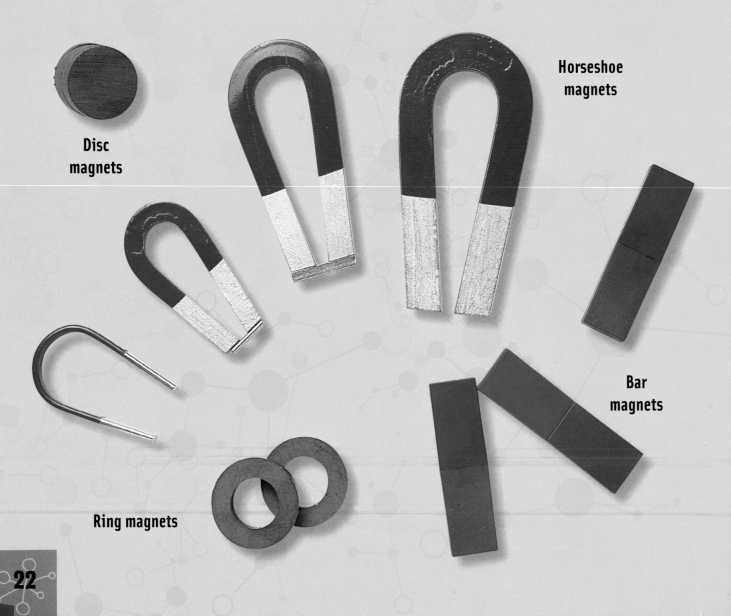

Disc magnets

Horseshoe magnets

Bar magnets

Ring magnets

South pole

Bring the south pole of a bar magnet towards one of the poles of the horseshoe magnet. If the two magnets push away from each other, the pole of the horseshoe magnet is a south pole. Two south poles are similar and so they repel each other.

The two south poles push away from each other.

North pole

Bring the south pole of the bar magnet towards the other pole of the horseshoe magnet. If the two magnets pull each other together, the pole of the horseshoe magnet is a north pole. The north and the south poles are opposite and so they attract each other.

The north pole and the south pole pull together.

How would you use a bar magnet to find the poles on a fridge magnet?

Test the force

Card is non-magnetic. A steel screw is magnetic. What will happen if you put card next to a magnet and a screw next to the card? Will the magnetic force still work through the card?

Equipment:

- steel screw
- pieces of card
- bar magnet

1.
Put a piece of card over the screw, then place the magnet over the card and lift it up. The magnetic force goes through the card and makes the screw stick to the card.

2.
Add another piece of card to test the strength of the magnetic force further. Place two pieces of card between the magnet and the screw. The screw still sticks to the magnet through the two pieces of card.

3.
Keep adding pieces of card to test the magnet's strength. How many pieces of card do you need to add before the screw falls away? Eventually, the force of the magnet will not be strong enough to pull through all of the pieces of card.

Equipment:

- bar magnet
- steel paper clips

The force at the poles

Have all parts of a magnet got a strong magnetic force? You can test this by putting a bar magnet on a table and covering it with steel paper clips.

If you lift up the bar magnet, the paper clips move towards the poles. The magnetic force is strongest at the magnet's poles.

Strength at the poles

One way to test the strength of a magnetic pole is to hang paper clips from it. Try it first with the north pole and then with the south pole. The more paper clips you can hang on to the magnet, the stronger the pole.

Test the strength of a range of magnets using pieces of card and a steel screw. Then hang a line of paper clips from each magnet. Which magnet is the strongest? Which is the weakest?

Using magnets

We use magnets every day. Inside a fridge door is a magnetic strip. When the door is closed, the strip makes the door grip the metal in the doorframe and holds it shut.

Compasses

A **compass** has a magnetic needle that is free to move. When you place it on a flat surface the needle is pulled into line by the Earth's magnetic field and it points north.

Hikers and explorers use the needle on a compass to find north and south. This helps them read a map and find their way.

Equipment:

- shoebox • ruler
- sticky tape • two pieces of
adhesive tack • magnet
- steel paper clip • thread

Make a hovering model

You can use a magnet to make a model of something hovering in the air.

1.

Stick the ruler to the shoebox with the sticky tape. Attach the magnet to the free end of the ruler with the adhesive tack.

2.

Loop the thread through the paper clip and attach the other end of the thread to the second piece of adhesive tack below the magnet. The magnetic force is greater than the pull of gravity on the paper clip and so the paper clip hovers in the air.

Using tissue paper, cut out a shape of your choice, such as white tissue paper in a cloud shape. You can attach your cloud to your hovering paper clip.

Glossary

Adhesive tack sticky substance used to join items together.

Attract make something come nearer.

Axis an imaginary line running through the centre of the Earth around which the planet spins.

Compass an instrument with a magnetic needle that moves to show the position of the North and South Poles.

Contact force a push or pull that occurs when one object touches another.

Force field a place where a non-contact force can push or pull on things around it.

Friction a force that acts between two surfaces which are touching each other. When one surface moves, a friction force pushes on it in the opposite direction.

Gravity a force that pulls objects down to the centre of the Earth. It also pulls planets around the Sun and the Moon around the Earth.

Gravitational pull the pull of gravity of a large object, like a star, on a small object, like a planet.

Magnetic used to describe something which is attracted to a magnet.

Magnetic material a material which is attracted to a magnet and can be made into a magnet. Iron and steel are examples of magnetic materials.

Non-contact force a push or pull that occurs between two objects that are not touching each other.

Non-magnetic material a material that is not attracted to a magnet. Pottery and wood are two examples of non-magnetic materials.

North and South Poles the places on the Earth's surface around which the planet spins. Think of the Earth as having a rod (we call it an axis) running through it and the planet spinning around it. The end of this rod at the top of the planet is called the North Pole and the end of the rod at the bottom of the planet is called the South Pole.

Planet a large spherical object made from rock or gases that moves around a star.

Pole the place at the end of a magnet where the magnetic force is sent out.

Repel push away.

Sliding friction a force that acts between two surfaces which are touching each other, whilst one surface is in motion.

Solar System the Sun and the planets, moons and asteroids that revolve around the Sun.

Star a huge ball of gases that gives out heat and light.

Static not moving, staying still.

Surface the top or upper layer of something.

Answers to the activities and questions

Page 5 What is a force?

Activity: You push the covers of the book to close it. You pull the covers of the book to open it.

Page 9 Gravity

Answer: The coins hit the tray at the same time. The force of gravity speeds up different-sized falling objects by the same amount.

Page 11 Friction

Answer: When cream is put on your hands they slide over each other more easily. This is due to the cream filling the tiny grooves in the skin, making the skin smoother and reducing friction at the same time.

Page 13 Investigating friction

Answer: The strongest force of friction is on the bumpy cardboard surface. The weakest force of friction is on the smooth wooden surface. The greater the friction between the car and the surface it runs on, the slower the car moves.

Page 15 Force fields

Activity: The North and South Poles of the Earth have a magnetic force like the two poles of a magnet. Your tracing should be a copy of the picture in the book with a bar magnet inside pointing to the North and South Poles. Note the geographic North and South Poles are the ends of the axis on which the planet turns. The magnetic north and south poles are not in exactly the same place, but for naming magnets and for finding your way you can think of them as the same place.

Page 17 Magnetic force

Answer: Lifting cars and waste metal in a scrap yard.

Page 21 Magnetic poles

Answer: They would push each other apart. Opposite poles attract each other. Similar poles repel each other.

Page 23 Finding the poles

Activity: Bring the north pole of the bar magnet up to the fridge magnet. If you feel a pushing force, you have found the north pole of the fridge magnet. If you feel a pulling force, you have found the south pole of the fridge magnet.

Page 25 Test the force

Activity: You may find that some magnets are stronger than others. You could make the test more accurate by using thin sheets of cardboard, instead of thick pieces. Scientists use different experiments to investigate the same thing.

Hang a line of paper clips from each magnet. The results from each experiment will give you more evidence to help you decide about the strength of the magnets.

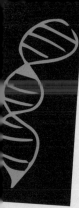

Index

About this book

Moving Up with Science is designed to help children develop the following skills:

Science enquiry skills: researching using secondary sources, all pages; grouping and classifying, pages 5, 15, 21 and 23; comparative and fair testing, pages 9, 23, 24 and 25.

Working scientifically skills: making careful observations, pages 5 and 25; setting up a practical enquiry, pages 19 and 21; making comparative or fair tests, pages 9, 23, 24 and 25; using results to draw simple conclusions, pages 11 and 19; using straightforward scientific evidence to answer questions, pages 9, 11 and 15.

Critical thinking skills: knowledge, all pages; comprehension, pages 13, 19 and 27; application, pages 5 and 23; analysis, page 15; synthesis, page 23; evaluation, pages 15 and 19.